Di...

BEDFORD

A MISCELLANY

Compiled by Julia Skinner
With particular reference to the work of Martin Andrew

THE FRANCIS FRITH COLLECTION

www.francisfrith.com

First published in the United Kingdom in 2006 by The Francis Frith Collection®

This edition published in 2014
ISBN 978-1-84589-758-1

British Library Cataloguing in Publication Data

Did You Know? Bedford - A Miscellany
Compiled by Julia Skinner
With particular reference to the work of Martin Andrew.

The Francis Frith Collection
6 Oakley Business Park,
Wylye Road, Dinton,
Wiltshire SP3 5EU
Tel: +44 (0) 1722 716 376
Email: info@francisfrith.co.uk
www.francisfrith.com

Printed and bound in England

Front Cover: **BEDFORD, HIGH STREET 1921** 70423p

The colour-tinting is for illustrative purposes only, and is not intended to be historically accurate

CONTENTS

INTRODUCTION

The first recorded reference to Bedford occurs as 'Bedanford' in a document of AD880; the name probably derives from 'Beda's Ford,' after an Anglo-Saxon leader who settled by the river. The Town Bridge has long superseded the original ford which gave the town its name, and which was guarded first by a Neolithic settlement, then a Danish encampment, and finally by a Norman castle.

Bedford was important enough to be selected as the chief town of Bedfordshire after this area of the country was won back by the English from the Danes in the late 10th century, and in the 11th century the town prospered as a trading centre and even minted its own coins. Architectural evidence of the pre-Norman town is scant but significant: it includes the present chancel of the church of St Peter de Merton, and some re-used stones and walling in St Mary's, south of the river. Bedford was awarded Borough status by Royal Charter in 1166, which confirmed the town's market and trading rights. The town's importance was centred on its position astride the navigable length of the Great Ouse at the confluence of roads that were later to become the A6, the A600 and A428. Such was the importance of the growing town as an administrative centre in the early Middle Ages that the Sheriffs of neighbouring Buckinghamshire used the castle in Bedford as their official seat for many years. The castle was destroyed in 1224 as the result of a siege by Henry III's forces against Falkes de Breaute, and all that now remains is the mound rising from behind the Bedford Museum in Castle Street.

Bedford was staunchly Parliamentarian during the Civil War of the 17th century. By the early 18th century the town was prospering as a trading centre, with the river acting as a trade artery, ferrying produce, coal and goods to the town's breweries, mills, warehouses

and factories. Daniel Defoe in the 1720s described Bedford as 'a large, populous, well-built and thriving town'.

Bedford expanded considerably in the 20th century, particularly to the east, absorbing several villages and large acreages of farmland, but the historic core of the town around the Ouse bridge is still recognisable from the photographs shown in this book, and Bedford is a pleasant place to visit. The river, once so vital to Bedford's trade, has now become a valuable leisure asset, and the town's parks and riverside walks more than compensate for the architectural losses, road development and suburban growth that have taken place in the last 50 years. The story of Bedford is full of fascinating characters and events, of which this book can only provide a brief glimpse.

THE RIVER AND THE BRIDGE 1921 70435

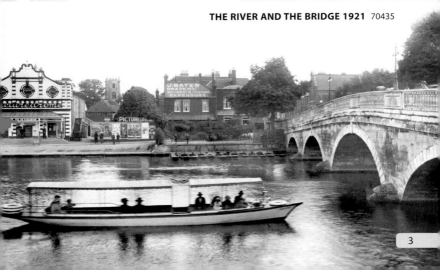

LOCAL DIALECT WORDS AND PHRASES

'Clodhoppers' - boots.

'Ferrcaling' - messing about with something.

'Clack' - mouth, thus 'clacking' is to chatter.

'Betty Bingo' - a fat woman.

'Nobby' - a fool.

'Jollop' - medicine.

'Grobbelers' - hands.

'Poor as Job's cat' - hard up.

'Buppy' - butter.

'Docky' - a mid-morning snack.

'Ockard' - awkward, meaning annoying or contrary.

'Dry as charff' - very dry, thirsty.

'Please Sirs' - Gypsies.

'Up the stairs to Bedfordshire' - going upstairs to bed.

HAUNTED BEDFORD

A ghost of a man is reported to wander the corridors of the higher floors of the main building of Bedford School at night, and on several occasions he has asked people who are in the building at night for directions to the exit; one boy who tried to assist found that when they had reached the door, the man had disappeared.

People working at offices in 38 Mill Lane reported in the mid 20th century that the building appeared to be haunted - strange footsteps and knocks on doors were heard.

In the Methodist Chapel in Newnham Avenue, the figure of a man in black trousers and a light tweed coat was reported by a witness in the mid 20th century as seen going through a wall, leaving a trail of white mist.

The junction of Tavistock Street, Union Street and Clapham Road is known as 'Black Tom's Grave' by many Bedford people. This was where the evil highwayman Black Tom was buried after being hanged; he was so feared by local people that he was buried with a stake driven through his heart to prevent him 'wandering'. However, this did not prevent his ghost haunting the area for many years, often accompanied with another, unidentified, phantom, and in the 1840s many people avoided the area at night for fear of meeting them. The last sighting of Black Tom was about 25 years ago, when a number of witnesses reported seeing a man with a swarthy complexion staggering along Union Street, head lolling as if his neck was broken. As they watched, the apparition faded away.

Willington Manor, four miles south of Bedford, is known for several mysterious phenomena; the sound of unexplained footsteps and the ringing of an unknown bell have been reported.

The King's Arms pub in Bedford is said to be haunted by the ghost of an unidentified young man.

BEDFORD MISCELLANY

The River Great Ouse was made navigable in the 1680s, and wharves, warehouses and stores appeared at Bedford. Coal, fish brought up-river in perforated trunks towed behind the barges, salt, millstones, tar, iron, timber and brick were landed at the wharves, while mainly agricultural produce such as wheat, malt, beans and apples in season were loaded for transport down-river. Coal was the main import in the 18th century, and brewing grew in importance as an industry.

Undoubtedly Bedford's most famous son - if only because of his imprisonment in the gaol there as the result of religious intolerance - is John Bunyan. He was born into a tinker's family and lived something of the high life before becoming a Nonconformist preacher after serving in the Parliamentary garrison at Newport Pagnell during the Civil War; he came to Bedford to seek religious guidance from John Gifford, the Puritan vicar of St John's Church, who was himself an ex-Royalist army officer and reformed rake. In 1660 he was arrested for preaching at Harlington, south of Ampthill, and spent the next 12 years in Bedford Gaol, sited at the corner of High Street and Silver Street (on the site of the Bedford Palace, seen in photograph 70423 on page 52-53). Released in 1672, when Charles II issued the Declaration of Religious Indulgence, he was later returned to gaol when the Declaration was rescinded, for not taking Church of England communion. A major outcome of his hardships was the writing and publishing of a religious parable, 'Pilgrim's Progress', although this was not the only work he produced. This has become one of the most successful books ever written, being published in over 200 languages.

John Bunyan

PRESENTED TO THE
BOROUGH OF BEDFORD
BY
HASTINGS IX DUKE OF BEDFORD
JUNE 10TH 1874
IN THE MAYORALTY
OF
GEORGE HURST, ESQ

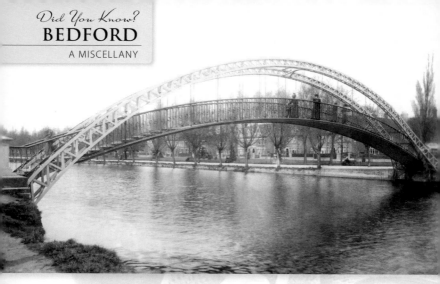

THE SUSPENSION BRIDGE 1898 40864

Most of Bedford's parks and gardens were laid out during Joshua Hawkins's mayoralty in the 1800s, and are wonderful assets for the town. Crucial to Hawkins's plans was the linking of the south and north banks of the Great Ouse, which was achieved by the graceful suspension bridge, shown in photograph 40864, above. The bridge was designed by John Webster and was opened in 1888. Popular with all Bedfordians, the bridge prevents a short stroll becoming a very long one. The ability to promenade from one bank of the river to another was further enhanced in 1998 with the opening of another bridge, known as the Butterfly Bridge, designed by Chris Wilkinson.

The 'Anglo-Saxon Chronicle' records for AD921 that a marauding Danish army reached Bedford, having ravaged the Huntingdon area: 'the (Bedford) garrison sallied out to meet them, fought against them and put them to flight, slaying a good part of them'.

One of Bedford's famous sons was the soldier, explorer and adventurer Frederick Gustavus Burnaby (1842-1885). He was born in Bedford and educated at Bedford Grammar School and Harrow, later joining the Royal Horse Guards. In the winter of 1876 he set off on a hazardous journey on horseback across the Russian Steppes. He later published an account of this adventure in 'Ride to Kiva'. He made a further journey through Asia Minor and Armenia in 1876-78, which he described in another book, 'Horseback Through Asia Minor'. He then changed his mode of travel and in 1882 became the first man to cross the English Channel alone in a hot-air balloon. He was foremost a soldier though, and was made a Colonel in 1881; he was killed at the battle of Abu Klea in the Sudan in 1885.

HIGH STREET c1955 B51139b

HIGH STREET 1921 70424

The motor agents' premises on the right of photograph
70425 on page 12 belonged to Murkett Bros, one of the
county's premier automobile companies which grew out of
an existing agricultural machinery business with its roots in
the 19th century.

At the Peace of Wedmore in AD878 between the Anglo-Saxon king,
Alfred the Great, and the Danish king, Guthram, the two sides agreed
to split the country into two areas of control: these were the Anglo-
Saxon kingdoms of Wessex and Mercia, and the Danelaw to the
north-east. The Danes were allowed to settle in the Danelaw and
Danish laws, not Anglo-Saxon, were followed. The Ouse formed part
of the agreed boundary; Bedford was in the Danelaw, whilst south of
the Ouse was in Anglo-Saxon territory.

In the early 1950s the London Brick Company instigated a labour recruitment drive in the southern Italian regions of Puglia, Campania, Calabria, and Sicily. Bedford became home to the largest concentration of Italian immigrants in the UK, and according to a 2001 census, 10% of Bedford's population is of Italian descent. Since 1954 Bedford has had its own Italian Vice Consulate. The cultural and social life of the town is enhanced by a wide variety of Italian bars, restaurants and social clubs as well as a large number of delicatessan and grocery shops selling Italian produce.

Lace-making was once an important cottage industry in Bedfordshire. The lace made here was 'Point Ground' lace, which was produced in the Lille style, with the pattern and ground being worked together. The lace made in Devon, in centres such as Honiton, was in the Brussels and Italian traditions, where the decorative elements are worked first and then finished off by 'grounding' them with connecting bars and mesh. The Bedfordshire lace-workers made the lace to orders via lace dealers.

The hand-made lace trade was seriously threatened when, in 1809, John Heathcoat (of Nottingham and later Tiverton), successfully developed a machine to make 'bobbin net', a ground material to which decorative elements could then be applied by hand. Later inventions led to machines capable of manufacturing lace through the complete process; although this machine-made lace was inferior to hand-made, it was cheaper and acceptable to the popular market, and the number of lace-workers in the Bedford area had fallen dramatically by the end of the 19th century, as shown by the 1891 Census. The making of Bedfordshire Pillow Lace has now become a recreational craft for people who are proud to keep alive this local tradition, and examples of Bedfordshire lace and other exhibits connected with the lace-making industry can be seen in Bedford Museum and the Cecil Higgins Art Gallery.

HIGH STREET FROM TOWN BRIDGE 1921 70425

After the death of King Alfred, his son, Edward the Elder, attempted
to win back the territory of the Danelaw. The 'Anglo-Saxon Chronicle'
for AD918 records that 'Jarl Thurcytel submitted to him and all the
Danish barons, and almost all the chief men who owed allegiance
to Bedford'. In AD919 'King Edward went with his army to Bedford
and occupied the fortress: most of the garrison who had previously
occupied it submitted to him. He remained there for four weeks, and
before he left he ordered the fortress on the south bank of the river
to be built.' Thus Bedford assumed its medieval shape on both sides
of the river; indeed, part of the King's Ditch, built for Edward, still
remains filled with water, but the stockades have long gone. These
entries are of great interest, for they show that the town existed well
before AD918 and that it was well fortified; they also give a precise
date for the southern expansion of the town.

In medieval times, although there was no direct road linking Bedfordshire's county town to London, one direct trade route, possibly a wool route, linked Cambridge, Bedford, Gloucester and Bristol. Technically that route still exists and it is possible to trace it out of Bedford westwards along the A422, north of Milton Keynes, across to Buckingham/Chipping Norton/Stow-on-the-Wold/Gloucester and then down the Roman road (A38) to Bristol.

Although there have been finds of Roman material such as coins in the Bedford area, there is little evidence of any substantial Roman settlement, although there was apparently a Romano-British community at nearby Kempston.

THE EMBANKMENT AND THE RIVER 1921 70443

Apart from John Bunyan, another great Nonconformist preacher, John Howard (1726-1790), stands in Bedford in statue form - see photograph 40860, opposite. John Howard, who lived at nearby Cardington, was twice Mayor of Bedford and Lord High Sheriff of the county in 1773. In his time Howard was derided for his views, particularly when they spilled from religion into politics - never comfortable bedfellows. Having been briefly imprisoned at Brest in France in 1756, he developed a lifelong passion for prison reform, and spent many years campaigning against conditions in the country's prisons and the indignities suffered by the inmates. His name and work live on in the Howard League for Penal Reform.

The individual parishes in Bedford found provision for the poor a heavy burden, which became worse as the town grew. In 1794 they secured a private Act of Parliament and established Incorporated Guardians who set up the town's workhouse, named rather curiously the House of Industry, which opened in 1796. The House of Industry became the Workhouse after the 1834 Poor Law Act. The building (by John Wing) survives as the core of Bedford General Hospital North Wing on Kimbolton Road.

St Mary's Church in Cardington has an extremely rare black basalt font, made by the Wedgewood factory in Stoke-on-Trent. It was given by Harriet Whitbread in 1783, and is one of only two Wedgewood fonts in England - the other is at Essendon in Hertfordshire.

THE HOWARD MONUMENT
1898 40860

JOHN HOWARD

1726–1790

1890

ELSTOW, BUNYAN'S COTTAGE 1921 39968

By the year 1200, Bedford had a river bridge with a nearby chapel,
a hospital (St John's, south of the river, which still retains its 13th-
century structure), a county gaol and two monasteries outside the
town, Newnham Priory to the east and Cauldwell Priory in Kempston
parish. Nearby to the south was the Norman foundation of Elstow
Abbey. Within the town there were several parishes: St Peter de
Dunstable, St Mary, and St John south of the river, the last in effect
the chapel to St John's Hospital, and to the north of the river were
the main church of St Paul, St Peter de Merton, and St Cuthbert,
besides the bridge chapel and the Herne Chapel. During the 13th
century the town acquired a Franciscan friary and a leper hospital,
St Leonard's Hospital, just outside the southern part of town on the
Ampthill road.

John Bunyan was born in Elstow, and lived in a cottage on Elstow High Street for four years after marrying his first wife. The Moot Hall in Elstow, shown in photograph 39967, below, dates back to the 17th century and now houses a most interesting museum which commemorate Bunyan's life. John Bunyan's home in the village (see photograph 39968, opposite) stood on the west side of the northern end of Elstow High Street, but was demolished in the 1960s. John Bunyan's works, of which 'Pilgrim's Progress' is the best-known, are celebrated in the Bunyan Trail. This 75-mile-long footpath winds through the Bedfordshire countryside linking elements of Pilgrim's journeys and the more factual aspects of Bunyan's life.

ELSTOW, THE MOOT HALL 1921 39967

From the 16th century, lace-making was taught to the children in local workhouses at Lace Schools, in order that they might earn something towards the cost of their keep. The Overseers of the Poor would pay an experienced lace-maker to teach the children, but they rarely received any other form of education, or learned other skills for future life: the Bedford Charity suggested that girls who had attended lace schools were 'generally unfit for household work'. The children worked a long and tiring day, and lace 'tells' were used to help relieve their boredom and help establish a routine for their work; these 'tells' were a form of chant which kept up the momentum of the lace-making, and were also a form of counting, either from 1 to 19 or 19 to 1. As the children sang out the 'tell', they changed the number of pins at each repetition until the 19th pin was reached, and then started again.

JOHN BUNYAN AND HIS COTTAGE E32501

The garden shown in photograph B51085, above, was situated
in the south-eastern corner of the grounds of Castle Mound.
Castle Close, but not the delightful garden, was incorporated
into a major redevelopment of the original location of Bedford
Castle.

After the Norman Conquest, Bedford underwent a radical change.
The south-east part of the north bank town was cleared to make
way for a large castle with a motte and bailey, which extended to St
Paul's Square. The motte, or castle mound, survives to the north of the
little park at Castle Close, and there is some 12th-century masonry
still to be seen. The castle saw action during the civil wars of the
12th century between King Stephen and the Empress Matilda, the
only legitimate heir of Henry I - there were sieges in 1137, 1141 and
in 1153, when Matilda's son Henry, later Henry II, captured it and the
town; after plundering the town, he 'delivered it to the flames'. More
peaceably, in 1166 the same Henry, now king, gave the rebuilt town
its Royal Charter which confirmed the rights and privileges granted
at an earlier time by Henry I.

**AMPTHILL
ST ANDREW'S CHURCH
c1955** A158011

A few miles south of Bedford is Ampthill. Henry VIII and his court paid many visits to Ampthill Castle, and the king brought his first wife, Catherine of Aragon, to Ampthill for the last years of their married life. The marriage was annulled in 1533 so that Henry could marry Anne Boleyn, and Catherine was proclaimed Princess Dowager. Ampthill Castle no longer exists, but Catherine's Cross stands in Ampthill Park as a memorial to the sad queen.

Catherine's Cross in Ampthill Park gained a measure of fame in the 1980s when it proved to be the burial site of the Golden Hare - the subject and prize of a national treasure hunt based on Kit Williams's book 'Masquerade'. The Golden Hare was eventually found just as the paperback edition of the book was about to be released, and a final chapter explaining how to decipher the clues was added. The position of the treasure had to be decoded from clues in a series of illustrations in the book, which eventually read: Catherine's/ long finger/ over/ shadows/ earth/ buried/ yellow /amulet /midday/ points/ the /hour/ in /light of equinox/ look you'. The first letter from each word or set of words from each picture spells 'close by Ampthill'.

In St Andrew's Church in Ampthill is a marble memorial to Colonel Richard Nicolls, who in 1664 captured the Dutch Colonial city of New Amsterdam on behalf of the English Crown, and then renamed it New York in honour of his commanding officer, James, Duke of York. The memorial carries a cannon ball in its base, which is said to be the one that killed Colonel Nicolls during the battle of Sole Bay in 1672.

The old Harpur School, now the Town Hall, was supplemented by the fine Tudor-style battlemented building seen in photograph 39933, opposite, when the Harpur Trust built the Modern School, or the Harpur Schools, in the 1830s. The building was designed by the renowned local architect John Wing, whose son was a pupil, but was completed by John Blore. No longer a school, it was preserved as a frontage block to a new shopping centre in the 1970s. The railings have long gone, but two of the ornate cast-iron lamp posts survive in what is now a pedestrianised street.

A Benedictine nunnery was founded at Elstow by Judith, Countess of Huntingdon, the niece of William the Conqueror, in the late 11th century. In later years the laxity and luxurious lifestyle of the nuns there was somewhat notorious; they were once criticised for their 'voided shoes', low-cut fashionable dresses with scarlet stomachers and stylish crested head-dresses. The abbey was dissolved by Henry VIII in 1539.

At the top of Silver Street is a bust of Reverend Trevor Huddlestone, who was born in Bedford in 1913. He was a tireless campaigner against apartheid in South Africa, to where he moved in 1943. In 1959 he helped found the anti-apartheid movement, and became its President in 1981, a role he held until his death in 1998. The bust in Bedford was unveiled in 2000 by Nelson Mandela, who said of Reverend Huddlestone: 'Father Huddlestone was a pillar of wisdom, humility and sacrifice to the legions of freedom fighters in the darkest moments of the struggle against apartheid.'

THE HARPUR SCHOOLS, HARPUR STREET 1897 39933

DE PARYS AVENUE 1897 39949

Bedford's trade was greatly helped by the 18th-century turnpiking of the main roads by turnpike trusts; these trusts charged a toll in return for making and maintaining decent highways. Most of these trusts date from the middle of the 18th century, for instance the Bedford to Hitchin Trust of 1757. Being a county town, Bedford always had a vigorous coaching trade and numerous coaching inns, with over 60 recorded in the mid 18th century, and the improved roads greatly aided this; for example, there were five coaches a day leaving the Swan Hotel for London in the 1820s.

Houghton House sits on a hill facing towards Ampthill, and is reputed to be the 'House Beautiful' of John Bunyan's 'Pilgrim's Progress'. Lady Pembroke built the house between 1615 and 1621, then the Bruce family bought it in 1624 and lived there for nearly 70 years. It came into the possession of the Dukes of Bedford in 1738, and in 1794 the Duke removed the roof and most of the fittings, for reasons which are not recorded. The staircase from Houghton House, carrying the date of 1688, is now in the Swan Hotel in Bedford. The ruin is now scheduled as an ancient monument.

HOUGHTON CONQUEST, HOUGHTON HOUSE 1897 39964

ST JOHN'S STREET 1921 70427

Photograph 70427, above, shows St John's Street. This part of Bedford was first developed after the Anglo-Saxon King Edward the Elder 'ordered the fortress on the south bank of the river to be built', in AD919. The photograph shows the view north along the street from approximately where Edward's defences crossed the road; this area is now the site of a large roundabout, with all the foreground buildings demolished.

In addition to Italian migrants (see page 11), in recent years Bedford has also absorbed a number of migrants from South Asia, Eastern Europe, Greece, Cyprus, the Middle East and Africa. It is now one of the most ethnically and linguistically diverse towns not only in Britain but also Europe. Over 100 immigrant languages are now spoken in Bedford, including Italian, Punjabi, Turkish, Polish, Portuguese and both Cantonese and Mandarin Chinese. 25 times as many languages in Bedford are spoken as in London, in proportion to population size.

Generations of Royal Air Force recruits will recognise the huts and airship sheds beyond the cabbage field in photograph C325013, below. The sheds were constructed during the First World War for the development of airships. Tall enough to contain Nelson's Column and long enough to hold an ocean-going liner, it is possible - in certain conditions - for condensation to fall as rain inside the buildings. During the Second World War and after, Cardington became part of Britain's air defence system, producing barrage balloons and training the personnel to handle them.

CARDINGTON, THE RAF BASE c1955 C325013

EMBANKMENT GARDENS c1955 B51027

Photograph B51027, above, shows Bedford's Peace Memorial in
Embankment Gardens. The names of those who died in both World
Wars and also the Korean War are not shown on the memorial, but
are inscribed on rolls held in the Borough archives.

During the Second World War, the BBC was evacuated to
Bedford. Stars of radio and stage became a frequent sight in
the town, and when the Americans joined the war Hollywood
stars were also a regular sight, including David Niven, Bob
Hope, Bing Crosby and many others.

Bedford School celebrated 450 years of independent education in 2002. Endowed by both the Harpur Trust and the Bedford School Trust, the former owns the school - and three others in Bedford - and the latter exists to hold certain funds and property for the general benefit. Sir William Harpur, a local merchant who subsequently became Lord Mayor of London, established the Harpur Trust with his wife Dame Alice in 1566 as an educational endowment, with any surplus going to the poor in Bedford. Sir William Harpur died in 1573; his memorial brass (and that to Dame Alice) is in St Paul's Church. The Bedford School Trust was established in 1926 and has been developed into a valuable source of funding, which is not dependent on fee income, for the school and those connected with it. Money is made available for a variety of purposes including building projects and the annual award of a number of scholarships.

BEDFORD SCHOOL c1955 B51139f

ST PETER'S CHURCH 1897 39941

The Church of St Peter de Merton, seen in photograph 39941, above, is of great interest, for it contains Anglo-Saxon work. The present chancel was the nave of the first church, while the tower was added after the Norman Conquest. Much of the rest of the church, the present nave and aisles to the left, are later medieval work with heavy Victorian restoration. The round-arched doorway to be seen on the left was re-erected here in the 1560s; it was salvaged from the demolished church of St Peter Dunstable on Cauldwell Street south of the river.

The medieval bridge over the river was replaced by the Improvement Commissioners set up by an Act of Parliament in 1803. Besides being empowered to replace the bridge, they also cleared away numerous houses near St Paul's Church and the medieval Guildhall in their zeal. The views of the river from the principal bedrooms of the elegant Swan Hotel were described by the diarist John Byng in the late 1790s as being highly agreeable with 'the smoothness of the wide water, the skipping of the fish, and the sight of a party of elegant female rowers'.

THE SWAN HOTEL AND THE RIVER 1898 40862

THE TOWN BRIDGE 1921 70434

The present Town Bridge was designed by the local architect John Wing. Its foundation stone was laid by the Marquess of Tavistock, the eldest son of the Duke of Bedford, in 1811, but the £15,000 building cost was a heavy burden on the town. By the time the bridge opened in 1813, it was done without ceremony: the local MP, Samuel Whitbread, merely walked across to meet the Commissioners and shake hands. A plaque on the downstream parapet records that the bridge was opened free of tolls in 1835 - the debt by then had been paid off.

John Bunyan's Independents bought a barn in Mill Street in 1672 to serve as the Bunyan Meeting Church, which was replaced by a church in 1707. The John Bunyan Museum is now a part of the Bunyan Meeting Free Church, owned and run by the members of that church.

In the 19th-century there was an icehouse under the northern part of the castle mound. Its central well, over 4m deep, would have been big enough to have held enough ice for all the inns in Bedford.

The Town Hall, on the west side of St Paul's Square, started life as a school, originally founded by Sir William Harpur in 1566. The left-hand part was the school, which was rebuilt in 1756 with a statue of Harpur in a niche. The porch with the turret and the parts to its right (seen in photograph 39930, below) were added in 1860 by a local architect, James Horsford, and now form the Bedford Civic Theatre.

THE TOWN HALL 1897 39930

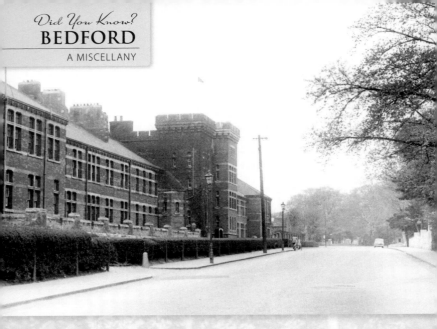

KEMPSTON, THE BARRACKS c1955 K96001

Kempston Barracks, the Regimental Depot of the 16th Foot, the Bedfordshire Regiment, was opened in 1876 and the first members of the Regiment arrived in May 1877. In 1918 it was designated as the Regimental Headquarters of the Bedfordshire and Hertfordshire Regiment. During the Second World War the Barracks was primarily a convalescent unit. Kempston Barracks, shown in photograph K96001, above, closed in 1958 and stood redundant for many years, although its fives courts were in use as a leisure facility at least until 1969. More recently the site has been given a new lease of life as a Masonic lodge, although part of the original Barracks, including the Keep, is to remain as a link to the Regimental War Memorial sited on the opposite side of Bedford Road.

The war memorial at Kempton, shown in photograph K96004, below, commemorates those serving members of the Bedfordshire and Hertfordshire Regiment who gave their lives during both World Wars and in conflicts from 1945 to 1958. The memorial consists of a small rotunda fronted by two pillars and a small garden of remembrance to the rear. On 11 November 1950 Her Majesty Queen Elizabeth (later the Queen Mother) unveiled the Book of Remembrance listing over 1,000 men of the Regiment who were killed during the Second World War. She was attended by an honour guard consisting of units drawn from the regular Regiment, the Territorial Army and the Bedfordshire and Hertfordshire affiliated units of the Combined and Army Cadet Force.

KEMPSTON, THE WAR MEMORIAL c1955 K96004

ST PAUL'S CHURCH 1897 39939

To the right of photograph 39939, above, is the old Floral Hall, which was demolished in 1904. It was built as the town's Corn Exchange in 1849, but was felt to be too small by the 1870s, when a new grander one was built on the north side of St Paul's Square.

The brand new spa centre at Bedford High School for Girls was formally opened in 2005 by a famous and successful past pupil - Dr Stephanie Cook OBE, Olympic gold champion in 2000 and World Champion in 2001 in the modern pentathlon event.

Straw-plaiting was formerly a cottage industry that employed many women and children in Bedfordshire. Straw was plaited for the hat-making industry, and also for items such as baskets, mats and ropes. The tools for this were a straw splitter, made of wood, bone or iron, which held cutters resembling miniature wheels with a varying number of razor-sharp spokes. In the middle of each wheel was a cone, on which each straw was centred before it was pushed through the cutter and sliced into the required number of splints. The sliced straws were pressed flat in a small mangle, which was usually fastened to the kitchen door. Then the plaiting started - the workers usually held the straws in their mouth. Different varieties of plait were given names, such as China Pear, Rock Coburg and Moss Edge. The finished plait was cut into lengths of about 20 yards. Most plaiters bought their straw from a plait dealer, a middleman who bought the straw from farmers. The finished plait was sold to agents of the Luton and Dunstable hat-makers. Women and children plaited to supplement a meagre family income. Boys as well as girls started plaiting at the age of four, or even earlier in some documented cases. In some areas children were sent to straw-plaiting schools, where they were often taught in the dark to accustom them to working without looking at the plait. The children were taught to plait with both hands whilst moistening the next straws in their mouth; consequently many children developed unsightly cracks at the corner of their mouths. A supply of straw was held under the left arm, leaving some children with a hunched left shoulder. Whilst lack of exercise led to stunted growth, catarrhal infections, sore mouths and crooked fingers were also occupational hazards.

THE SUSPENSION BRIDGE 1921 70446

Bedford's castle endured its last siege in 1224 when the young king, Henry III, was outraged by the seizure of one of his judges, Henry de Braybrooke, by the castellan, the over-mighty subject par excellence, Falkes de Breaute. The siege was described in lingering detail by a bloodthirsty monk at Dunstable Priory, and is one of the best contemporary sources for a medieval siege. It lasted eight weeks, and included the excommunication of the garrison by the Archbishop of Canterbury during the siege, and their hanging afterwards. The castle was slighted to prevent it being of further military use, and some of the stonework was used in repairs to St Paul's Church and other Bedford buildings.

Girl straw-plaiters making ropes for use on farms used to work on the roof of St Michael's Church in Millbrook, near Ampthill, feeding their plaited rope over the parapet of the tower as it grew longer. The girls worked until the end of their plait reached the ground, at which time they stopped work for the day. As they worked they recited this work song:

> *'Over one and under two,*
> *Pull it tight and that will do'.*

St Cuthbert's Church was possibly of Anglo-Saxon origin. The church seen in photograph 39944, below, was rebuilt in 1847; the architect, Woodruffe, chose the Norman style, which enjoyed a brief vogue before the Gothic Revival triumphed everywhere in Victorian England. The church is now a Polish Roman Catholic church serving Bedford's sizeable Polish community.

ST CUTHBERT'S CHURCH 1897 39944

The demographics of Bedford changed during the 18th century. Up until then, most citizens had landholdings scattered throughout large open fields; those who did not let out their holdings were part-time farmers as well as following other occupations, such as lace merchants, butchers, brewers or drapers. The enclosure of the open fields, undertaken by private Acts of Parliament, reached a crescendo in the second half of the 18th century, and allowed for more efficient farming. Thanks to agreements made among the more significant landowners, the widely distributed strips and small fields were replaced by centralised holdings of larger fields. This not only facilitated better farming practice, but also opened up the possibility of expanding the town - this had been impossible with the dispersed holdings of the medieval strip-farming system. Bedford's Enclosure Acts enclosed the fields of St Paul's, St Peter's and St Cuthbert's parishes north of the river in 1797 and St John's parish south of the river in 1799. Thus the town was poised in 1800 to expand beyond the ancient bounds into the surrounding countryside; much of this development got under way by the 1860s, partly led by the prosperous townsmen, who now gave up living over, by or behind their shops, breweries, warehouses and businesses, and built themselves villas in the new suburbs.

Tradition says that when Queen Catherine of Aragon, Henry VIII's divorced first wife, was living at Ampthill, she had an effect on the Bedfordshire lace-making industry: some stories say that she actually began the local industry by teaching local women to make lace, others that the established industry was going through a decline and the queen ordered all her lace to be burnt and commissioned new, to give work to the local lace-makers. A form of bobbin lace, 'Catherine of Aragon's lace', was named after her, and for many years afterwards the lace-makers would set aside a small sum of money to provide cakes to be eaten on St Catherine's Day, 25 November, in memory of the patron saint of lace-makers and also of the queen.

Bedford contains the headquarters of the Panacea Society, who are the guardians of the famous box left by the prophetess Joanna Southcott (1750-1814). The society reminds the world of the box through newspaper advertising: 'War, disease, crime and banditry will increase until the Bishops open Joanna Southcott's box'. The box allegedly contains writings which will banish all these ills from the world, but under the terms of the will the box can only be opened in the presence of 24 bishops, who have so far declined to co-operate. The box, called the Ark of the Testament by the Society, contains the Lord's teachings and advice on how to cope with the devastation and danger that is foretold in the Bible, particularly in the Book of Revelations.

NEWNHAM OUTDOOR POOL c1960 B51081

SPORTING BEDFORD

Bedford has always had a very strong rugby tradition. The rugby club was founded in 1886, and even before the turn of the 20th century the club had played prestigious fixtures against the Barbarians and Stade Francais. The team of the mid 1960s was one of Bedford's finest, producing (amongst others) two England captains, David Perry and Budge Rodgers. Another high point was Bedford's victory in the 1975 Knockout Cup, when they beat Rosslyn Park in the final at Twickenham.

Bedford Town FC has never reached a very high level, even in the non-League football world. However the club did achieve a degree of national acclaim for its giant-killing acts in the FA cup, most notably in the 1950s. The club beat a succession of League teams including Watford, Norwich, Newcastle, Exeter and Brighton. But perhaps the club's finest hour ended in a glorious defeat. In 1955/56 they were drawn to play Arsenal at Highbury. In front of 55,000 people they forced a 2-2 draw with the north London giants, and were only four minutes away from victory in the replay. Sadly, the Eagles lost 2-1 after extra time.

One of Bedford's most famous athletes is surely Paula Radcliffe. She was brought up in the town, becoming a member of Bedford Athletics Club. An athlete of the highest calibre, by December 2005 she had run four of the five fastest marathons of all time. She has also won a string of the world's top marathon races, including the New York, Chicago and London marathons.

Bedford's tradition of fine athletes goes back to the early 20th century, and a particular star was Harold Abrahams, born in Bedford in 1899. He won the Olympic 100m gold medal in Paris in 1924, and was part of a silver medal-winning relay team. Abraham's success was depicted in part in the 1981 film 'Chariots of Fire'.

Rowing sports have always played a large part in the leisure activities of Bedford's citizens, and the Bedford Regatta each May is Britain's largest one-day rowing event. There are 2 amateur rowing clubs, Bedford Rowing Club and Star Club, which has produced a number of international athletes, including Olympic champion Tim Foster, who won Olympic gold in 2000 at Sydney in the coxless four alongside Steve Redgrave, Matthew Pinsent and James Cracknell.

QUIZ QUESTIONS

Answers on page 49.

1. An urn in the Embankment Gardens has a plaque giving the information that it was presented to the people of Great Britain by 'The Stone City of the World'. Where is the Stone City?

2. Who is Dame Alice Street named after?

3. Where in Bedford can you find a bull standing on a clock?

4. How does a plaque on the old Corn Exchange on the north side of St Paul's Square commemorate Bedford getting 'In the Mood'?

5. John Bunyan is commemorated in Bedford with a fine statue on St Peter's Green at the north end of the High Street, seen in photograph 40857 on page 7. This was by the noted sculptor Sir Edgar Boehm, and was presented to the town by the 9th Duke of Bedford in 1874. What can be seen around the base of the statue?

6. There is a statue of William Harpur in a niche in the façade of the former Harpur school in St Paul's Square, which is now the Town Hall - but how is this statue historically incorrect?

7. The Peace Memorial in the Embankment Gardens is surmounted by a knight standing on what?

8. The statue of John Howard in Bedford, of 1890, is by one of England's finest Art Nouveau sculptors, Alfred Gilbert. Which famous statue in London is also Gilbert's work?

9. Where can you see good and evil angels struggling for possession of a child?

10. What was the flat top of the mound of Bedford Castle used for in the 16th century?

RECIPE

BEDFORDSHIRE WIGS

These cakes were traditionally eaten on 25 November, St Catherine's Day, which was believed to herald the beginning of winter.

Ingredients

450g (1lb) black treacle
100g (4oz) butter
300ml (½ pint) milk
450g (1lb) plain flour

100g (4oz) sugar
1 teaspoon bicarbonate of soda
2 teaspoons ground ginger
15g (½oz) caraway seeds

Melt the treacle and butter together in a thick saucepan. When the mixture is hot, stir in the milk. Put all the other ingredients into a bowl and make a well in the centre. Stir in the syrup mixture and blend thoroughly together. Pour into several shallow round cake tins and bake at 180 degrees C/350 degrees F/Gas Mark 4, for 30 minutes. The mixture will rise over the edge of the tins so that the thick rum looks like the curl of a wig.

RECIPE

BEDFORDSHIRE CLANGERS

This traditional dish has always been known as Bedfordshire Clangers, although only one large roll is made. Nowadays it takes the form of a pasty with a savoury filling at one end and a sweet filling at the other, but originally both meat and fruit were incorporated into the dish together.

Ingredients for the pastry:
450g/1lb suetcrust pastry
1 egg, beaten
Granulated sugar

For the savoury filling:
1 small onion, finely chopped
1 tablespoonful oil
225g/8oz minced pork
1 teaspoon dried sage
1 cooking apple, peeled,
cored and diced

50g/2oz cooked peas
Salt and pepper

For the sweet filling:
2 dessert apples, peeled,
cored and diced
Grated rind and juice of one orange
2 tablespoonfuls caster sugar
50g/2oz stoned dates, chopped
50g/2oz sultanas

First make the savoury filling: fry the chopped onion in the oil until soft. Add the pork and sage and cook gently for ten minutes, stirring often. Add the chopped apple after five minutes. Stir in the peas after ten minutes and remove from the heat. Leave aside. Make the sweet filling by mixing all the ingredients together thoroughly.

Roll out the pastry and cut into two 25cm (10 ins) circles. Using trimmings cut a 25cm (10 ins) strip of pastry and lay it across the centre of one circle, making it hold with a little beaten egg. Brush the edge of the circle with beaten egg. Hold the pastry circle with both hands grasping the ends of the dividing line of pastry. Lift the two edges and pinch together, pinching the dividing line too, to make a wall of pastry across the centre of the pastry. Fill one side with half the savoury filling, and the other side with half the sweet filling. Pinch the pastry edges firmly over them, forming a conventional pasty shape. Glaze with beaten egg, and sprinkle with sugar. Make a second pasty with the remaining ingredients in the same way, and bake at 220 degrees C/425 degrees F/Gas Mark 7, for 15-20 minutes or until crisp and golden.

QUIZ ANSWERS

1. Bedford's namesake - Bedford, Indiana, in the United States of America. The urn was presented in 1948 by the Indiana Limestone Co Inc.

2. Alice Harpur, wife of William Harpur. The couple were important benefactors to the town, establishing the Harpur Trust.

3. Over John Bull (jewellers) in High Street there is a clock surmounted by a figure of a bull. It can be seen in photograph 70424 on page 10.

4. A plaque and bust on the building commemorate the fact that Glenn Miller and his orchestra were billeted in Bedford during the Second World War, and played for dances in this building. 'In the Mood' was one of their most popular numbers.

5. Around the plinth of the statue are bronze panels showing scenes from Bunyan's famous book, 'Pilgrim's Progress'.

6. The statue shows William Harpur dressed in 18th-century clothes, rather than the Tudor costume which would be historically correct, as he lived in the 16th century.

7. The knight on the memorial is standing on a prone dragon.

8. Alfred Gilbert was also responsible for the statue of Eros in Piccadilly Circus in London.

9. In the Cecil Higgins Art Gallery - this is the title of a pen and watercolour work by William Blake (1757-1827). The Gallery has a fine collection of around 600 of the best known images and examples of work of leading artists from the late 16th century to the 1980s, including Hogarth, Gainsborough, Turner, Constable, Cotman, Blake, Millais, Rossetti, Landseer, Whistler, Beardsley, Gwen John, Sickert, Lowry, Hepworth, Nicholson, Henry Moore and Freud.

10. The flat top of the mound was used as a bowling green. A fragment of a white ceramic bowling 'jack' was found during archaeological excavations of the south side of the mound.

HIGH STREET 1921 70423

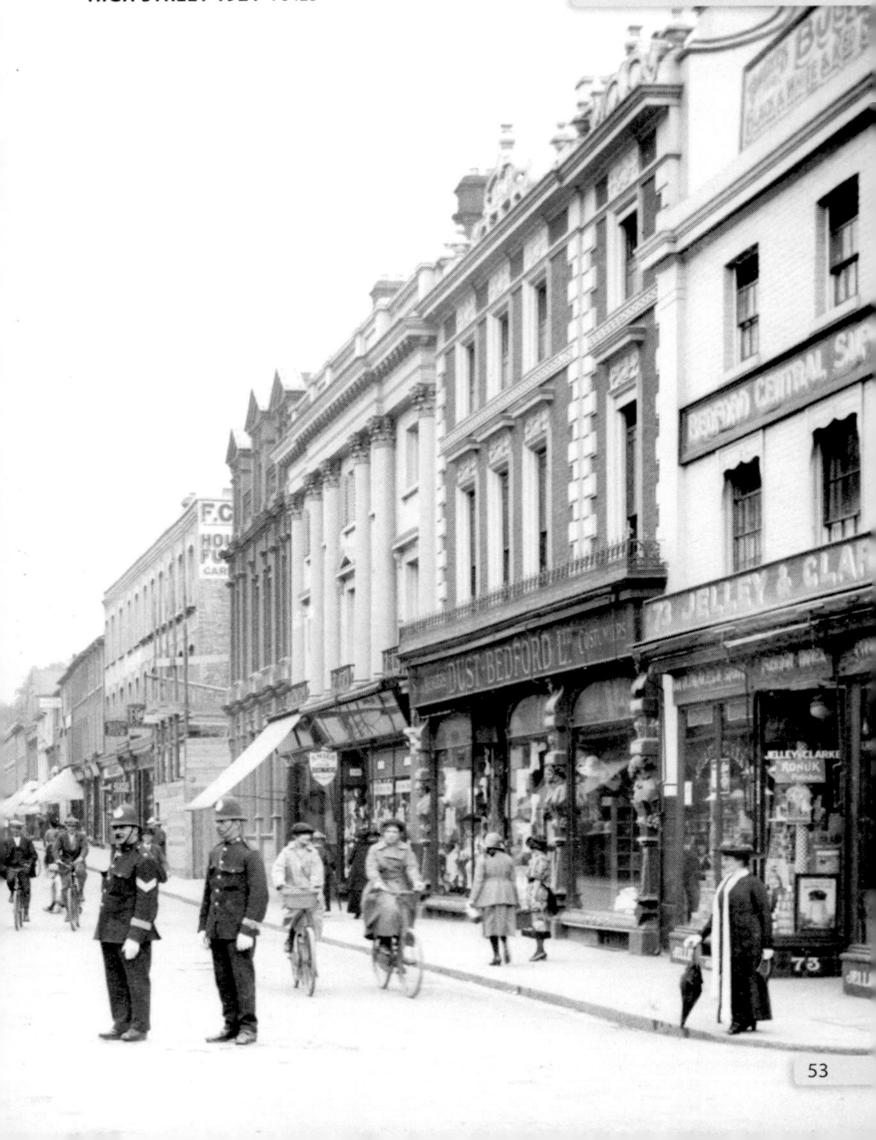

FRANCIS FRITH

PIONEER VICTORIAN PHOTOGRAPHER

Francis Frith, founder of the world-famous photographic archive, was a complex and multi-talented man. A devout Quaker and a highly successful Victorian businessman, he was philosophical by nature and pioneering in outlook. By 1855 he had already established a wholesale grocery business in Liverpool, and sold it for the astonishing sum of £200,000, which is the equivalent today of over £15,000,000. Now in his thirties, and captivated by the new science of photography, Frith set out on a series of pioneering journeys up the Nile and to the Near East.

INTRIGUE AND EXPLORATION

He was the first photographer to venture beyond the sixth cataract of the Nile. Africa was still the mysterious 'Dark Continent', and Stanley and Livingstone's historic meeting was a decade into the future. The conditions for picture taking confound belief. He laboured for hours in his wicker dark-room in the sweltering heat of the desert, while the volatile chemicals fizzed dangerously in their trays. Back in London he exhibited his photographs and was 'rapturously cheered' by members of the Royal Society. His reputation as a photographer was made overnight.

VENTURE OF A LIFE-TIME

By the 1870s the railways had threaded their way across the country, and Bank Holidays and half-day Saturdays had been made obligatory by Act of Parliament. All of a sudden the working man and his family were able to enjoy days out, take holidays, and see a little more of the world.

With typical business acumen, Francis Frith foresaw that these new tourists would enjoy having souvenirs to commemorate their days out. For the next thirty years he travelled the country by train and by pony and trap, producing fine photographs of seaside resorts and beauty spots that were keenly bought by millions of Victorians. These prints were painstakingly pasted into family albums and pored over during the dark nights of winter, rekindling precious memories of summer excursions. Frith's studio was soon supplying retail shops all over the country, and by 1890 F Frith & Co had become the greatest specialist photographic publishing company in the world, with over 2,000 sales outlets, and pioneered the picture postcard.

FRANCIS FRITH'S LEGACY

Francis Frith had died in 1898 at his villa in Cannes, his great project still growing. By 1970 the archive he created contained over a third of a million pictures showing 7,000 British towns and villages.

Frith's legacy to us today is of immense significance and value, for the magnificent archive of evocative photographs he created provides a unique record of change in the cities, towns and villages throughout Britain over a century and more. Frith and his fellow studio photographers revisited locations many times down the years to update their views, compiling for us an enthralling and colourful pageant of British life and character.

We are fortunate that Frith was dedicated to recording the minutiae of everyday life. For it is this sheer wealth of visual data, the painstaking chronicle of changes in dress, transport, street layouts, buildings, housing and landscape that captivates us so much today, offering us a powerful link with the past and with the lives of our ancestors.

Computers have now made it possible for Frith's many thousands of images to be accessed almost instantly. The archive offers every one of us an opportunity to examine the places where we and our families have lived and worked down the years. Its images, depicting our shared past, are now bringing pleasure and enlightenment to millions around the world a century and more after his death.

For further information visit: www.francisfrith.com

INTERIOR DECORATION

Frith's photographs can be seen framed and as giant wall murals in thousands of pubs, restaurants, hotels, banks, retail stores and other public buildings throughout Britain. These provide interesting and attractive décor, generating strong local interest and acting as a powerful reminder of gentler days in our increasingly busy and frenetic world.

FRITH PRODUCTS

All Frith photographs are available as prints and posters in a variety of different sizes and styles. In the UK we also offer a range of other gift and stationery products illustrated with Frith photographs, although many of these are not available for delivery outside the UK – see our web site for more information on the products available for delivery in your country.

THE INTERNET

Over 100,000 photographs of Britain can be viewed and purchased on the Frith web site. The web site also includes memories and reminiscences contributed by our customers, who have personal knowledge of localities and of the people and properties depicted in Frith photographs. If you wish to learn more about a specific town or village you may find these reminiscences fascinating to browse. Why not add your own comments if you think they would be of interest to others? See **www.francisfrith.com**

PLEASE HELP US BRING FRITH'S PHOTOGRAPHS TO LIFE

Our authors do their best to recount the history of the places they write about. They give insights into how particular towns and villages developed, they describe the architecture of streets and buildings, and they discuss the lives of famous people who lived there. But however knowledgeable our authors are, the story they tell is necessarily incomplete.

Frith's photographs are so much more than plain historical documents. They are living proofs of the flow of human life down the generations. They show real people at real moments in history; and each of those people is the son or daughter of someone, the brother or sister, aunt or uncle, grandfather or grandmother of someone else. All of them lived, worked and played in the streets depicted in Frith's photographs.

We would be grateful if you would give us your insights into the places shown in our photographs: the streets and buildings, the shops, businesses and industries. Post your memories of life in those streets on the Frith website: what it was like growing up there, who ran the local shop and what shopping was like years ago; if your workplace is shown tell us about your working day and what the building is used for now. Read other visitors' memories and reconnect with your shared local history and heritage. With your help more and more Frith photographs can be brought to life, and vital memories preserved for posterity, and for the benefit of historians in the future.

Wherever possible, we will try to include some of your comments in future editions of our books. Moreover, if you spot errors in dates, titles or other facts, please let us know, because our archive records are not always completely accurate—they rely on 140 years of human endeavour and hand-compiled records. You can email us using the contact form on the website.

Thank you!

For further information, trade, or author enquiries
please contact us at the address below:

The Francis Frith Collection, Oakley Business Park, Wylye Road, Dinton, Wiltshire SP3 5EU.

Tel: +44 (0)1722 716 376 Fax: +44 (0)1722 716 881
e-mail: sales@francisfrith.co.uk **www.francisfrith.com**